# A
# *Glimpse of*
# DARTMOOR
---
# FOLKLORE
---

Belinda Whitworth

*Peninsula*
*Press*

The map of Dartmoor on pages 16-17 is reproduced with the kind
permission of the Dartmoor National Park Authority.

Illustrations by Brian Ainsworth.

Published by Peninsula Press Ltd
P.O. Box 31
Newton Abbot
Devon TQ12 5XH

Tel: 0803 875875

Printed in England by D.D.S. Colour Printers, Weston-Super-Mare.

ISBN 1 872640 08 7

# A GLIMPSE OF DARTMOOR
# · FOLKLORE ·

## Contents

# Introduction

With its lonely uplands, isolated homesteads, windswept rocks and chattering streams, Dartmoor has been described as the last wilderness in southern Britain. Its rich history goes back to earliest times, with evidence of prehistoric, Celtic, Saxon, medieval and later settlement.

Its folklore is equally extraordinary.

In the following pages you will find malicious and mysterious pixies, Dewer the ferocious huntsman with his eerie Wisht Hounds, 'hairy hands', rocks that dance, pools that speak, witches and phantoms, charms, omens and superstitions.

If this whets your appetite for more, then as well as visiting the area for yourself and meeting its inhabitants you might like to look at some of the books on page 32 or even consult classic Victorian texts by Dartmoor's first folklorists such as the Reverend Sabine Baring-Gould, William Crossing and Mrs Bray.

The maps referred to in this book are: Ordnance Survey Outdoor Leisure: Dartmoor (2½ in to 1 mile) - Ordnance Survey Landranger 191: Okehampton and North Dartmoor (1¼ in to 1 mile) - Ordnance Survey Landranger 202: Torbay and South Dartmoor (1¼ in to 1 mile). In the text the numbers of the last two maps precede relevant map references to show on which of the two maps you will find a particular place, e.g. 'the Nine Maidens (191/614928)' means that you will find the Nine Maidens on Landranger map 191 and the grid reference is 614928.

## The Author

Belinda Whitworth has lived in Devon since 1976. A freelance book editor and writer, she is also the author of *Gothick Devon* (Shire 1993). She is a member of several different local, national and international environmental organisations.

◆

# Ghosts

# The Hairy Hands

This macabre story is unique to Dartmoor and unusual in that all the events took place this century, in the 1920s, although similar legends have been in existence in the area for a very long time.

On an innocuous-looking stretch of the B3212 at Bellever Forest (191/646788 to 635771) between Postbridge and Two Bridges a series of inexplicable and sometimes fatal accidents began. Carts overturned, bicycles went out of control, horses shied and cars skidded. Finally, an army despatch rider, after a motorcycle crash, told of a pair of hairy hands that had seized the handlebars and wrenched his bike off the road.

By this time, the authorities decided to do something, and the camber of the road was altered.

A few years later on a moonlit night in a caravan near the same spot a woman awoke to see a large hairy hand clawing at the window. In her terror she made a sign of the cross, and the hand vanished.

One explanation of the hands is that they belong to an 'elemental', a semi-formless being, or to a crash victim haunting the area. Another, that they are echoes of past violence - the area was thickly populated in the Bronze Age.

Whatever they are, they seem now to have gone to ground ... or have they?

# The White Bird of the Oxenhams

Many of Dartmoor's ghost stories are obviously the results of overactive imaginations or the reworking of stereotypes. This chilling legend is one of the few that seems to have suffered little in the way of distortion or embellishment since its origins, and is truly mysterious.

The Oxenhams came to Dartmoor in the sixteenth century. Oxenham Manor (191/665943), now much altered, is in South Tawton, on the northern edge of the moor.

There was a tradition going back to the early middle ages that the death of one of the family was heralded by a white or white-breasted bird.

The most famous incident concerns 'Lady' Margaret Oxenham. At a feast on her wedding eve her father saw a white bird hovering over her head. The next day in the church a rejected suitor stabbed her to death.

There are reliable written accounts of sightings from the seventeenth century onwards. Among them is one in the British Museum and the Bodleian Library at Oxford dated 1641. This refers to four members of the family who died and says that witnesses to the appearance of the bird 'were not by any rewards hired to speak so' and were examined for the truth of their testimony by a minister.

The last written evidence describes the death of an Oxenham in 1873 when the bird was seen by someone who had no knowledge of the tradition. Finally, just before the First World War, neighbours of an Amyas Oxenham who was living in Exeter say they saw a white dove fly in through his bedroom window shortly before his death. Amyas's son went to live in Canada and there are even reports that the bird was seen across the Atlantic.

The direct family line is now extinct.

# Lady Howard of Fitzford

My Ladye hath a sable coach
With horses two and four
My Ladye hath a gaunt blood-hound
That goeth on before.
My Ladye's coach hath nodding plumes
The driver hath no head.
My Ladye is an ashen white
As one that long is dead.

A more baroque story this time, and perhaps less credible. Because of supposed crimes during her lifetime, Lady Howard's ghost is condemned to travel every night from Fitzford House in Tavistock to Okehampton Castle (191/585942) on the King's Way moorland track via Lydford. At Okehampton the dog must pluck a blade of grass and take it back home and only when all the grass has been removed from the castle's grounds can the lady rest in peace.

In some versions of the story Lady Howard rides in the coach, in others she is herself the 'gaunt blood-hound', a black creature sometimes with one eye and sometimes with two. The story doesn't specify why the driver should be headless.

The legend probably refers to a seventeenth-century Lady Mary Howard. However, although her father was apparently extremely dissolute and responsible for at least two murders, she herself was not evil, just forceful. It is possible that she has been confused with a Lady Frances Howard at the court of James I who was sent to the Tower for poisoning two of her four husbands.

There is a Lady Howard's Walk in the grounds of Okehampton Castle and the gateway of Fitzford House still stands. The poem is part of a ballad recorded by the folklorist the Reverend Sabine Baring-Gould (in *Songs of the West*) at the turn of the century.

# ⬛ *Ponies, Pigs, Goats and Dogs* ⬛

Wild ponies have ranged across the moor since prehistoric times but phantom ponies do not seem to have appeared much before this century.

On Gidleigh Tor (191/672878) during the Second World War the sound of hooves thudded close by two members of the Home Guard but no animal ever materialized.

In the 1960s a group of ponies was heard on Petticoat Lane leading into Throwleigh (191/667908) and a rush of wind was felt, but again nothing was seen.

A motorist drove straight through a pony in Hart Hole Lane going down to Dartmeet. The animal vanished into thin air and the car was undamaged.

An old and rather sad tale is that of the phantom sow and her starving litter who travel fruitlessly in search of food between Merripit Hill (191/658803) and Cator (191/680760).

A headless goat was seen in the 1930s in the lane leading to Wallabrook Bridge (191/653871) and one has also been seen several times near Postbridge.

If there is any connection between these goats and the animal sacrifice probably used by the moor's early inhabitants then this distressing apparition may have originated thousands of years ago.

Stories of ghostly black dogs, and packs of hounds in particular, are found all over Europe and Dartmoor is no exception. Here they are called the Wish, Wist or Wisht ('wisht' being an old word for eerie), Yeth or Heath Hounds and frequent in particular Wistman's Wood and the Dewerstone (SX538639) (see also page 25).

Other mystery dogs have been seen on the B3212 between Moretonhampstead and Postbridge and between Princetown and Plymouth, at Okehampton Castle (191/585942) - perhaps this is Lady Howard's ghost (see page 7), above Pizwell (191/669785) and at many other places all over the moor. A white dog has been seen on Cator Common (191/670770).

Probably the most famous of these creatures is the fictional 'hound of the Baskervilles'. Conan Doyle used to stay near Buckfastleigh and no doubt heard the story of the town's Squire Cabell who was so wicked that when he was buried the Wisht Hounds came to howl at his tomb. Grimpen Mire in *The Hound of the Baskervilles* is thought to be based on the treacherous Foxtor Mires (202/610700).

# Witches

# Witches and Hares

Witches are supposed to be able to change form and there are several Dartmoor stories, mostly rather nasty, about witches turning into hares. The following is a typical example.

A poor old woman heard that a local hunt was offering sixpence to anyone who could put up a hare for them. She told her grandson that she would predict where a hare was to be found and he must then tell the hunt.

In this way the old woman managed to earn several sixpences, but the hare was never caught, and the hunt began to get suspicious. One day after they managed to wound the hare they followed it into the old woman's cottage where it had fled. Inside they found no hare but instead the old woman in bed, dressing a large wound in her leg, in exactly the same place as the hare's wound had been.

This time they had no proof but later, for bewitching a young woman and making her spit pins, the old woman was burnt at the stake.

Hares have long had supernatural associations. Along with black dogs, they are supposed to haunt three-way crossroads, a particular feature of Devon and Dartmoor. A symbol consisting of three hares or rabbits in a circle was used by the moor's tinners and decorates the roofs of some of the moor's churches, such as Widecombe and North Bovey.

# Vixana

Vixana was a witch who lived on Vixen Tor. She used to enjoy luring travellers to their death in the bogs which then surrounded the tor by calling down mists to confuse them. One day a man who had been given a ring by the pixies to make him invisible and who could see through mists crept up behind her and pushed her off the rocks to her death.

Vixen Tor (191/542743) is near the B3357 between Tavistock and Two Bridges, and there is a footpath from Merrivale. From the road the tor looks like a man and woman on horseback but from nearer to it looks like the head of an old woman.

# Witchcraft Yesterday and Today

### Charm for burns

*Three Angels came from North, East and West*
*One brought fire, another brought frost*
*And the third brought the Holy Ghost.*
*So out fire and in frost.*
*In the name of the Father, Son and Holy Ghost.*

Some say witchcraft is derived from ancient pagan religions whose followers, men as well as women, worshipped nature, particularly the sun and moon, and practised crop fertility rites.

It is possible that Dartmoor's standing stones were used in some of these early rituals. Charcoal has been found in the centre of some of the larger circles, suggesting that they were used for ceremonial fires.

Sheep sacrifice was practised on the moor until last century and ram-roasting festivals were carried out at menhirs (single standing stones). These may have been some of the last public demonstrations of the 'old religion'.

If witchcraft did exist, it must have been forced underground by Christianity, but its practices would have lingered in out-of-the-way places like Dartmoor. Some of the legends attached to the moor's prehistoric remains, such as the Nine Maidens (see page 20), may point to these unorthodox religious activities.

Right up until this century Dartmoor had a strong tradition of charms and curses, many of them, like the one above (from *Folk Rhymes of Devon* by William Crossing), a fascinating mixture of 'superstition' and Christianity. Not long ago a large coil of human hair was found in a cist (a stone tomb) on the moor, proof perhaps of even more recent activity.

# Pixies

*There's piskies up to Dartymoor*
*And t'idden gude yu sez there b'aint.*

Just as Ireland has its leprechauns and Scandinavia its trolls, so Dartmoor has its pixies.

There are innumerable stories about them. 'The Tulip Pixies' is one of the most charming, whereas 'The Magic Ointment' illustrates the darker side of the pixy character.

# The Tulip Pixies

Not far from Tavistock on the edge of the moor was a cottage with a pretty garden full of flowers. At night the woman who lived there would wake to the sound of sweet music, and the tulips she had planted gave off a scent more lovely than that of honeysuckle or roses.

The ability to see pixies is given to few but one evening at dusk as the woman looked out of her window she saw pixies bringing their babies and laying them each in a tulip flower to sleep. The woman realized that it was the pixies' breath that was scenting the flowers and the music was the lullabies they sang.

When the woman died the cottage was bought by a man who uprooted all the flowers so that he could plant vegetables. The pixies were heartbroken and left the garden, never to return. Soon it was a desolate waste as nothing would grow there any more.

With loving care the pixies tended the woman's grave instead, making sure that the turf was always neat and green and that beautiful flowers grew there all year round.

No one ever saw them but sometimes at night people would hear sad singing and know that it was the pixies mourning their departed friend.

There is a modern sequel to this story in Kitty Jay's Grave (see page 22) where a mystery pot of flowers is always found.

# The Magic Ointment

One stormy night a Tavistock midwife was woken by a violent banging on her door. On her doorstep she found an ugly little man holding a large black horse with eyes of fire.

"Come quickly", he said, "My wife needs your help."

Reluctantly she mounted the horse behind the man and allowed herself to be blindfolded.

Eventually they arrived at a cottage and the midwife assisted at the birth of the woman's baby. The mother asked the midwife to rub some ointment on the baby's eyes. Out of curiosity the midwife then secretly rubbed some on one of her own eyes. Instantly the mother was transformed into a beautiful fairy-like lady and the baby was wrapped in silver gauze.

The next day as she went to market she saw the little man again and went up to speak to him. He was astonished that she could see him and asked which eye it was that she saw him with. He then struck the offending eye and caused her to be blind in that eye for the rest of her life.

In another version of the story a Holne midwife takes the ointment home with her by mistake and there tries some on one of her eyes. This time it makes everything seem larger than normal, but unnaturally clear, with the stars shining even though it's daytime. Unhappily the conclusion is the same.

# *Habits and Haunts*

Although they can be kind, pixies are more often mischievous, even malicious. They are almost always secretive.

Sometimes they are dressed in rags, sometimes in colourful doublet and hose. Sometimes they are slim and fairy like, sometimes like miniature wizened people.

Some of them help about the house and people leave bowls of milk or water out for them. Others take horses by night and return them in the morning, lathered and exhausted. Some even steal children.

But their favourite activity is dancing and you can often see the circles of extra-green grass they leave behind.

To be 'pixy-led' is to lose your way and become confused, like John Fitz (see page 23). One of the few remedies is to turn your coat or your pockets inside out as quickly as possible.

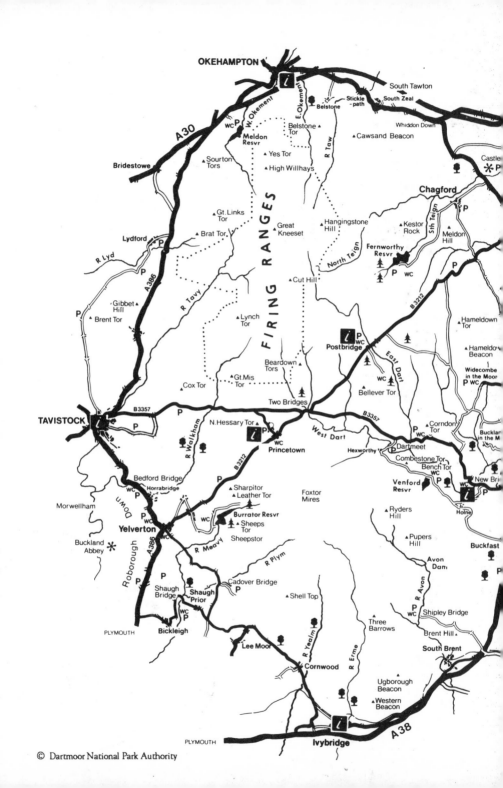

© Dartmoor National Park Authority

# DARTMOOR

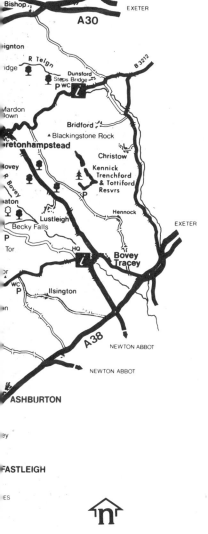

As well as grassy swards, pixies also use the moor's prehistoric stone circles for their revels and many other places have special associations with the 'little people'.

*New Bridge* (202/712708) - a picturesque medieval bridge between Holne and Holne Chase where pixy revels have been heard at night.

*Pixies' Cave or House* (202/567681) - a narrow granite cave below Sheepstor (202/566682), used by Cavalier fugitives during the Civil War.

*Pixies' Cross* (191/534742) - one of the moor's ancient stone crosses, over seven foot high.

*Pixies' Holt* (191/668733) - a rock passage some four feet wide and thirty-seven feet long near Dartmeet, 'holt' meaning a hollow.

*Pixies' Parlour* - a tumble of boulders on the footpath between Fingle Bridge (191/743899) and Sandy Park (191/712896) where pixies meet and dance.

*The Puggie Stone* - an enormous boulder on the banks of the River Teign near Holystreet (191/688878) with a strong tradition as a pixy meeting-place; the name is related to Puck, the arch-pixy.

There are documented sightings of pixies right up to the present day but it has been suggested that legends about pixies and similar beings are folk memories of actual races that disappeared or were driven by invaders to remote woods and caves.

Some archaeologists believe that there was an early type of human being even smaller than pygmies. Dartmoor itself has been inhabited since the Stone Age by successive groups of people including bronze-users and Saxons, and possibly Celts as well.

# *People*
# *and Places*

# The Nine Maidens

## (191/614928)

*And now at every Hunters Moon*
*That haggard cirque of stones so still*
*Awakens to immortal thrill,*
*And seven small maids in silver shoon*
*'Twixt dark of night and white of day*
*Twinkle upon the sere old heath*
*Like living blossoms in a wreath,*
*Then shrink again to granite grey.*

There are two versions of the delightful legend attached to this group of standing stones on Belstone Common.

The more usual belief is that the stones dance every day at noon. In his poem above (from *Book of Avis*) Eden Phillpotts, the Dartmoor novelist, describes the stones coming to life once a year at Hunter's Moon (the first moon after the full moon nearest to the autumn equinox - which is about 23 September).

A discrepancy will be noticed in the number of stones. This is not surprising as according to superstition no two counts of standing stones are ever the same. The optimum figure here seems to be sixteen or seventeen.

Dartmoor is littered with prehistoric remains - stone avenues, stone tombs ('cists'), single standing stones ('menhirs') and circles. The full story behind their purpose will probably never be known but the smaller circles, such as this one, usually encircle burial mounds.

There is a tradition that it is dangerous to tamper with any of the stones and William Crossing, the Dartmoor historian, records that when a cist (191/734755) at Widecombe was opened by a former parson his house was destroyed by an explosion the following night.

Scorhill stone circle (191/655874) on Gidleigh Common, one of the larger ones, has the reputation of scaring horses and riders have to make a detour.

And why the name? Folklore has it that the maidens were turned to stone for dancing on the sabbath. Perhaps there is a confusion here between the 'sabbath' and witchcraft 'sabbats' or ritual festivals (from the old French 's'esbattre' meaning 'to frolic'). Nine has a tradition as a 'magical number' and because of the sun and moon the circle would have been an important feature of bygone nature worship and witchcraft.

Maybe it is not really the stones that dance on Belstone Common after all.

# Crazywell Pool
## (202/582705)

This lonely expanse of water, over an acre in area, lies on the high moor between Sheepstor and Princetown.

It is said that at various times in the past a voice has been heard calling loudly from the water with the name of the next person in the parish to die. For this reason people who worked on the moors would walk several miles out of their way rather than pass anywhere near it.

Another version of the superstition maintains that an image of the next person to die will appear in the pool on midsummer's eve.

Recently two local youths were challenged to spend midsummer's eve at Crazywell. As they rode home later that night the motor bike they were on failed to negotiate a bend on Roborough Down and both were killed.

What had they seen in the pool? Their own reflections?

Legend also has it that the River Dart claims lives, one per year, and can be heard calling for its victim beforehand. Hence the old rhyme:

*River of Dart, O river of Dart,*
*Every year thou claimest a heart.*

Supernatural phenomena are often associated with water and there is a theory that the special electrical field of water acts as a kind of tape recorder of strong emotions. Underground water was possibly of the greatest importance to prehistoric people in the siting of their monuments.

Dartmoor has innumerable rivers and streams, much boggy terrain that is sometimes watery, eight reservoirs and several flooded mines, but no natural lakes or pools. Although Crazywell Pool is the result of tin working it is distinguished from other artificial waters on the moor by the hidden spring that feeds it.

# Jay's Grave, Childe's Tomb and Fitz's Wells

### (191/732798, 202/618703, 191/592939 and 191/577758)

The first two of these well-known features illustrate the grimmer side of Dartmoor's past, prettified by folklore.

The pitiful story of Kitty or Mary Jay takes place in the eighteenth century. A servant girl and orphan, abandoned by her lover and carrying his child, she hanged herself.

She was buried near Manaton where three parish boundaries meet as none would claim responsibility for her, at a crossroads so that her spirit would not be able to find its way back to its former haunts and bother anyone. (One arm of the crossroads is now a footpath.)

In about 1860 the spot was disturbed by a road mender and the bones of a young woman found. The man reburied these in a coffin and restored the grave. Since then the grave is always decorated with a pot of flowers, although no one admits to putting it there.

In a local television programme in 1978 a young woman under hypnosis appeared to recall a previous life as Kitty Jay and described in harrowing detail the last few weeks of the orphan's life.

Childe was a hunter caught in a blizzard at nightfall on the desolate and deadly Foxtor Mires (202/610700). In desperation he slaughtered his horse and huddled inside the still-warm carcass for protection. To no avail however for his body was later found frozen to death at the spot where his monument now stands.

Sadly nothing of his 'tomb' - rectangular granite blocks topped with a rough granite cross - is original as the site was restored at the end of last century. Beneath it however is a chamber which may be a prehistoric tomb.

It is thought that the protagonist was either a fourteenth-century Amyas Childe or the eleventh-century son of a Saxon earl of Devon, 'Childe' deriving from 'cild', a Saxon title of honour.

The body was found by monks and there is a story that before the Second World War two girls visiting the area and apparently knowing nothing of its history saw a party of monks with a bier approaching their car. They switched off their engine and waited for the procession to pass but as it came level with them it vanished.

A cross with a different purpose is that marking Fitz's Well near Okehampton. This is supposed to be a holy well and anyone who drinks from it on Easter Sunday will be married within a year or have good luck for a year. Unfortunately the well is now covered.

John Fitz, the grandfather of Lady Howard whose ghost rides out nightly from Fitzford House, put up the cross in the sixteenth century.

There are stone crosses all over the moor, the majority thought to be medieval waymarks. Some of these ancient tracks such as the Abbot's Way (from Buckfast Abbey in the east to Buckland Abbey in the west) and the Lich Way (from Bellever to Lydford) still exist and can be found on maps.

There is another Fitz's Well near Princetown, sometimes called Fice's Well. Here John Fitz put a canopy over a spring, and on it the initials I[J]F and the date, 1568, can still just be seen.

According to legend Fitz and his wife were 'pixy-led' while out on the moor but restored by drinking from the wells. He erected the memorials in gratitude.

# Lydford

*I oft have heard of Lydford Law*
*How in the morn they hang and draw*
*And sit in judgement after.*

Twelfth-century Lydford Castle used to be a prison for offenders against Dartmoor's strict hunting and tin-working laws. Judge Jeffreys, notorious for his harshness, is said to haunt it in the shape of a black boar.

People from far into the moor had to bring their dead to Lydford Church for burial, travelling along the Lich Way ('lich' meaning a body, alive or dead). Small wonder that phantom funeral processions are sometimes seen making their way along the ancient track.

In the sixteenth century the caves of the steep and rocky gorge below the castle sheltered a degenerate tribe of thieves called the Gubbins who terrorized the area. Charles Kingsley, who was born at Holne, wrote about them in *Westward Ho!*

At one end of the gorge is a dark pool of swirling water called the Devil's Cauldron and at another pool called Kit's Steps the ghost of an old lady in a red headscarf has been seen.

In spite of its sombre past Lydford today attracts many visitors.

# Spinsters' Rock
## (191/700908)

This neolithic burial chamber is the only example of its kind in Devon and probably the oldest prehistoric monument on the moor.

According to legend its three seven-foot-high granite rocks with their sixteen-ton stone 'lid' were put up by a band of stalwart lady spinners (not necessarily unmarried) one morning before breakfast.

Although the structure did collapse in 1862 and has been re-erected, it is difficult to see any meaning in the legend. One possibility is that the 'spinners' are related to Belstone's 'maidens' (see page 20) and the name is a veiled reference to witchcraft.

There is a tradition on the moor that standing stones will fall on to faithless wives and flatten them. Perhaps there is another connection here!

'Ley' hunters say that Spinsters' Rock stands on one of these straight energy lines through natural features and ancient monuments. It is also claimed that it was built to mark a meeting place of underground springs, an especially sacred place to prehistoric people.

# Bowerman's Nose
## (191/742804)

On Hayne Down near Manaton, a short walk from the road, rises an unmistakable tor with the profile of a bulbous-nosed man in a peaked cap.

At one time people believed that the tors were massive religious sculptures like the stone figures on Easter Island, put up by the Celtic priesthood, the Druids. On many of the tors are loose basin-shaped rocks which the Druids were supposed to have made for catching the blood of their sacrifices. The lines and cracks in the tors were a form of writing.

Scientists however say that the tors are natural granite outcrops and that all their features can be explained by the action of weather.

Usually in Dartmoor's legends the witches are worsted and the huntsmen are all powerful. Thankfully the roles are reversed here.

Bowerman was a 'bowman' who disturbed a coven of witches. In revenge they turned him and his hounds to stone. The hounds can be seen at nearby Hound Tor (191/742790) and sometimes on dark nights you can still hear them baying.

Alternatively, the name comes from the Celtic *vawr-maen*, 'great stone'.

# The Dewerstone

(SX538639)

In the far south-western corner of the moor above the meeting place of the Rivers Plym and Meavy is an awesome crag said to be the home of Dewer, Dartmoor's phantom huntsman. With his fearsome Wisht Hounds (see pages 8-9) he pursues lone travellers over the sheer rock face to their death below. The foot of the rock is haunted by a black dog.

Cloven hoofed and horned, Dewer is a figure with counterparts in many cultures. To Christians he is the devil and hunts the souls of unbaptized babies.

A farmer, coming home late at night somewhat the worse for wear, met up with the demon huntsman. Not realizing who he was he asked him what he had caught that day.

Laughing, the huntsman handed over his catch telling the farmer to keep it.

The farmer hurried off, thinking with pleasure of the good supper he was going to have that night.

When he got home he unwrapped the bundle and found inside it not some tasty small animal or bird but instead the dead body of his own child.

Enough to turn anyone back to the straight and narrow.

# Sayings and Superstitions

To cure shingles make a wreath of rushes, put it over the affected area of skin and then hang it up inside a chimney. Do this three times.

To get rid of chilblains you should wish them on to someone just dead.

A collar of woven ash twigs or a hazel wand put round the neck of an animal bitten by an adder will cure it.

Snake skin will repel thorns so if you have a thorn on one side of your finger put some snake skin on the other side.

Don't keep kittens born in May because when adult they will bring in snakes.

Where an adder lies hidden, a dragonfly hovers above.

Drawing a witch's blood, even that from a pin prick, will break any spell cast by that witch.

The first direct glance from a black witch contains the malevolent influence so you must divert this by wearing bright buttonholes or hanging up things like coloured glass balls, bunches of flowers or branches with lots of berries.

Witches must not discuss their power or it will leave them. Nor must they accept money, for the same reason.

Beware of the wych elm - it is used in witchcraft.

Dill, vervain, mountain ash, St John's wort, trefoil, elder, garlic, verbena, bracken and pennywort all guard against evil influences.

Setting fire to growing ferns produces rain.

If a circle is drawn round a hen and the bird is then carried round it with its beak to the circumference it will stay in the circle.

Will o' the wisp is the spirit of an animal that has sunk into the bog and died.

Lambs must not be tailed when the moon is waning as the bleeding will not stop until the moon has 'turned'.

Don't pick stitchwort or you run the risk of being 'pixy-led'.

The ringing of church bells is a good way to deter pixies.

*He who in July the cuckoo's voice doth hear*
*Will die before he comes another year.*

To hear the first cry of the cuckoo on your right is lucky; on your left unlucky.

Gelding should be carried out on Good Friday and children weaned, but no clothes washing should be done or one of the family will be 'washed clean' (die) before the year is out.

*She who cuts dough with a knife*
*Will ne'er be happy, maid, widow or wife.*

# Calendar

**TWELFTH NIGHT** - (5/6 January)
Wassailing in orchards - singing, drinking cider and making noise to scare away evil spirits and ensure plenty of apples later in the year

**CANDLEMAS** - (2 February)
First of four main witches' sabbats (and Church festival)

**LADY DAY** - (25 March)
Fairs for hiring workers

**COLLOP MONDAY** - (Monday before Lent)
Collops (slices of meat), eggs and pancakes eaten

**LENSHARD DAY** - (Tuesday before Lent)
Children called at houses for pancake ingredients and threw broken crockery
(Lent 'shards') in the doorway of anyone who didn't contribute

> *Pan kakes an' fritters*
> *Us be come for,*
> *If you don't give us some,*
> *Us'll bang down the door*

**EASTER**
Fitz's Well, Okehampton, visited
Sunrise service on Yes Tor (191/580902)

**BELLEVER DAY** - (soon after Easter)
Beginning of a week's hare hunting on Bellever Tor (191/644764)

**TAIL-PIPE DAY** - (1 April)
Tomfoolery such as attaching notices to other people's backs

**MAY DAY/BELTANE** - (1 May)
Beacons lit on hills
Second of four main witches' sabbats
Dancing tree celebrations at Moretonhampstead - a platform was put in a sacred
tree and people danced on it. Similar celebrations at many sacred trees.
*Maypole dancing

**STINGING-NETTLE DAY** - (3 May)
Children beat each other with nettles

**BEATING THE BOUNDS** - (1st Monday after 3 May at Bovey Tracey)
Villagers walked round parish boundaries beating the boundary stones with sticks.
Conducted in many other parishes at different times.

**OAK-APPLE DAY/GARLAND DAY** - (29 May)
People decorated themselves and their houses with oak apples and oak leaves
General festivities

**WHITSUN** - (7th week after Easter)
Fairs and games, especially at Widecombe

**TRINITY** - (8th week after Easter)
Fairs and games
Gooseberry pasties and cream traditional fare at Drewsteignton
*Drinking, dancing and skittles at Meavy Oak

**MIDSUMMER'S DAY** - (24 June)
Fire and water ceremonies and a time for seeing into the future
Sheep sacrifice at Buckland
Ram roasting at Holne (also possibly on 5/6 July)
Rolling of a burning wheel at Buckfastleigh

**BEATING THE BOUNDS** - (17 July)
At Buckfastleigh

**LAMMAS** - (1 August)
Third of four main witches' sabbats
Also called Feast of the First Fruits

**\*ASHBURTON ST LAWRENCE FAIR** - (10 August)
Dating from at least fourteenth century with bull baiting, ale tasting, bread
weighing and pig droving

**BEATING THE BOUNDS** - (last week in August)
At Gidleigh

**\*MORETONHAMPSTEAD FAIR** - (last week in August)

**\*WIDECOMBE FAIR** - (2nd Tuesday in September)

> *Tom Pearse, Tom Pearse, lend me your grey mare,*
> *All along, down along, out along, leigh,*
> *For I want to go to Widecombe Fair,*
> *All along, down along, out along, leigh.*

*With Bill Brewer, Jan Stewer, Peter Davey, Peter Gurney,*
*Daniel Whiddon, Harry Hawk, Old Uncle Tom Cobley and all,*
*Old Uncle Tom Cobley and all*

World famous because of the traditional song and a very popular event

## MICHAELMAS - (29 September)
'Giglet' fairs for hiring workers

## *TAVISTOCK GOOSE (OR GOOSEY) FAIR
(Until last century on Michaelmas Day, 29 September, now 2nd Wednesday in October)

At least eight hundred years old. Roast goose was traditional Michaelmas fare. Thousands of geese would be driven to Tavistock and then on to London, with shoemakers en route to make small soft leather shoes for any geese that became lame. Today it draws people instead. Nineteenth-century roundabout, funfair and livestock auctions.

## HARVEST
'Crying the neck' - ceremonial gathering in of last sheaf of corn

## HALLOWE'EN - (31 October)
Eve of pagan new year
Fourth main witches' sabbat

## ST ANDREW'S DAY - (4th Thursday in November)
Feasting and sports at Moretonhampstead

## CHRISTMAS - (25 December)
'Ashen faggots' (ash twigs and branches bound together) were burnt in homes
Mumming plays at Ashburton and Bovey Tracey

* These events still take place in one form or another. There are many fairs and festivals at villages and towns throughout the moor from March to November. For up-to-date information see the free annual newsheet *The Dartmoor Visitor*, available from local public libraries, or contact the Dartmoor National Park Headquarters, Haytor Road, Bovey Tracey, Devon TQ13 9QJ, telephone 0626 832093.

# Books

Copley, Len, and Gant, Tom *Dartmoor Legends Retold* (Baron Jay nd)
- *More Dartmoor Legends and Customs* (Baron Jay nd)

Coxhead, J R W *Legends of Devon* (Western Press 1954)
- *Old Devon Customs* (Raleigh Press 1957)
- *Devon Traditions and Fairy Tales* (Raleigh Press 1959)
- *The Devil in Devon* (West Country Handbooks 1967)
- *Ghosts in Devon* (Town and Country Press 1972)

Devon Folklife Register *Folk Festivals and Traditions of Devon* (Exeter City Museums Service 1980)

Farquharson-Coe, A *Devon Witchcraft* (James Pike 1975)

Grinsell, Leslie V *Folklore of Prehistoric Sites in Britain* (David & Charles 1976)

Hippisley Coxe, Antony D *Haunted Britain* (Hutchinson 1973)

Leger-Gordon, Ruth St *The Witchcraft and Folklore of Dartmoor* (Robert Hale 1965)

Pegg, John *After Dark on Dartmoor* (John Pegg 1984)
- *The Face of Dartmoor* (John Pegg 1988)

Starkey, F H *Dartmoor Crosses and Some Ancient Tracks* (F H Starkey 1983)
- *Odds and Ends from Dartmoor* (F H Starkey 1984)

Weir, John (ed) *Dartmoor National Park* (Webb & Bower/Michael Joseph 1987) (Countryside Commission official guide)

Whitlock, Ralph *The Folklore of Devon* (Batsford 1977)

Wilson, Colin (intro by) *Westcountry Mysteries* (Bossiney Books 1985)

Wreford, Hilary, and Williams, Michael *Mysteries in the Devon Landscape* (Bossiney Books 1985)